What they don't tell you about

PIRATES

OF THE PAST

This b[...]
who would have nicked it anyway.

Hodder
Children's
Books

a division of Hodder Headline plc

AHOY THERE ME HEARTIES!

This here book is about pirates and their
wicked plundering ways. BE WARNED! Us pirates
got up to some VERY NASTY TRICKS – HAH! HAH!
So if you're a faint-hearted, lily-livered scaredy-cat
you should put this book back on the shelf right
now! Otherwise...

WELCOME ABOARD, SHIPMATES!

Copyright © Lazy Summer Books 1995

The right of Lazy Summer Books to be identified as the authors of the work
has been asserted by them in accordance with the Copyright, Designs and
Patents Act 1988.

Text by Jim Hatfield
Illustrated by Thompson Yardley
Produced by Lazy Summer Books for Hodder Children's books

Cover portrait of Blackbeard courtesy of the National Maritime Museum,
Greenwich

10 9 8 7 6 5 4 3 2 1

Published by Hodder Children's Books 1995

ISBN 0340 63623 8

Hodder Children's Books
a division of Hodder Headline plc
338 Euston Road, London NW1 3BH
Printed and bound by Cox & Wyman Ltd, Reading, Berks
A Catalogue record for this book is available from the British Library

CONTENTS

 Whenever you see this sign in the book it means there are some more details at the FOOT of the page, like here.

PIRACY

WOULD YOU MAKE A GOOD PIRATE?

Do you think pirates were people with wooden legs, parrots and eye-patches who lived long ago in a far-off part of the world? Well, you're right, but only half right. 'Pirate' is an old Greek word which means a 'sea-going robber' – and there are still plenty of them around.

Pirates have come in all shapes and sizes, but mugging people at sea is what they all have in common. Nobody likes to admit the seas aren't safe. It's bad for business. So they don't talk about pirates much. Pirates keep quiet too, because they don't want to get caught. It's all rather secret.

Here are some common questions answered...

WHY DID THEY DO IT?

- Some governments permitted pirates to rob 'enemy' ships. These sorts of pirates were called privateers. Sir Francis Drake was a privateer.

- Some pirates were runaway sailors who couldn't stand ship's discipline, or they were escaped prisoners, or slaves on the run from their owners. Some of the original buccaneers were like this.

- Some pirates just wanted the money.

5

WHO WERE THE FIRST PIRATES?

There have been pirates as long as there have been sailors. The first pirates we know of worked in the Mediterranean and preyed on the Egyptian, Phoenician and Greek merchants who used to trade in precious goods.

WHAT DID THEY NEED TO GET STARTED?

- a ship to sail in
- a target ship with plenty of booty on board
- lots of fellow pirates, armed to the teeth, to help overpower the victim
- a safe haven where they could spend their booty

How did they die?

If things went well, pirate life could bring in a lot of money. On the other hand, pirate life was dangerous, bloody and very, very short!

Pirates died in many ways:

- fighting the crew of a treasure ship
- being caught and hanged
- being executed by rival pirates
- after quarrelling with other pirates
- shipwreck and drowning
- catching a horrible disease
- drinking too much.

Take your pick!

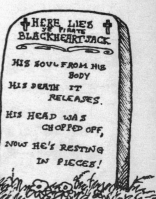

HERE LIES
ye PIRATE
BLACKHEART JACK

HIS SOUL FROM HIS
BODY
HIS DEATH IT
RELEASES.
HIS HEAD WAS
CHOPPED OFF,
NOW HE'S RESTING
IN PIECES!

Was there a special pirate personality?

The ideal pirate had to be:

- greedy
- tough
- cruel
- a bit crazy
- dirty
- and very quarrelsome

WAP!

COULD **YOU** BE A PIRATE?

I. WHAT SORT OF LEG-WEAR DO YOU LIKE?

a) A kilt with pink leg warmers
b) Jeans with flower patches
c) Leather trousers covered in dried blood

2. WHAT FOOD DO YOU LIKE?

a) Warm bone marrow from a freshly killed cow
b) Smoked salmon with a sprig of parsley
c) Shredded wheat and chips

3. WHAT DO YOU LIKE TO DRINK?

a) Iced tea with a dash of lemon
b) Rum and gunpowder
c) Ribena

THE RIGHT ANSWERS:

1) c 2) a 3) b

Score 10 points for each right answer.

0 points – what a wimp. No chance of becoming a pirate.

10 points – maybe you could take up flower arranging instead!

20 points – promising pirate material with a bit of on-the-job training.

30 points – smart! First class pirate!

WHAT DID PIRATES LOOK LIKE?

Most people have the wrong idea about what pirates were really like. People dream about what it would be like to live outside the law, and not have to live by rules. So there are lots of stories about romantic, handsome pirates, such as Errol Flynn in the film 'Captain Blood'. Well you can forget all that soppy nonsense about romantic, handsome pirates. You're going to find out about the real thing. Real pirates could be a pretty ugly bunch. Take Captain John Ward in 1808 for example. A commentator at the time described him as being...

> short with little hair, and that quite white, bald in front; swarthy face and beard. Speaks little, and almost always swearing – drunk from morn till night.

John Ward and Errol Flynn – which is the real pirate?

Read on for Cap'n Ebenezer Pegg's Guide to Pirates of the Past. But first, let's get kitted out... ➡

CATALOGUE OF PIRATE CLOBBER

1 headband
1 baggy cotton shirt
1 pair of baggy trousers
1 wooden leg
1 eye patch
1 leather belt with brass buckle
1 parrot
1 nose ring
2 ear-rings
1 hook
1 cutlass
1 pistol
1 spyglass
1 neckerchief
1 knee-length boot
1 sea chest
1 torn map
1 bottle of rum

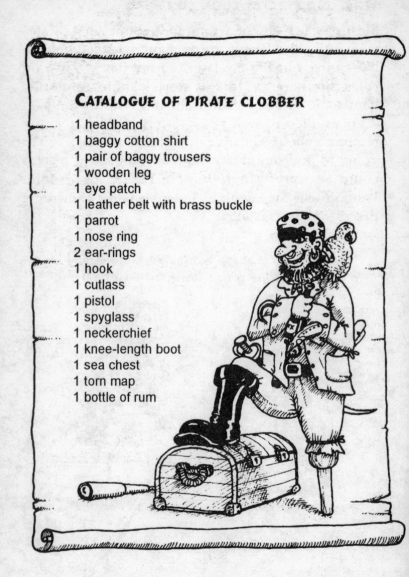

PIRATES OF THE PAST

CAP'N EBENEZER PEGG'S GUIDE TO PIRATES

PIRATE TIME-LINE

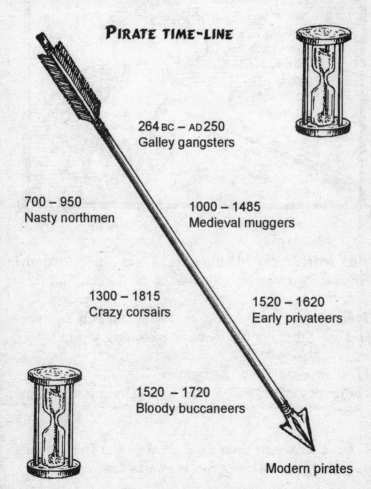

264 BC – AD 250
Galley gangsters

700 – 950
Nasty northmen

1000 – 1485
Medieval muggers

1300 – 1815
Crazy corsairs

1520 – 1620
Early privateers

1520 – 1720
Bloody buccaneers

Modern pirates

GALLEY GANGSTERS

WHEN? 264 BC – AD 250

WHERE? They operated in the Mediterranean, Black Sea, Red Sea and Arabian Sea.

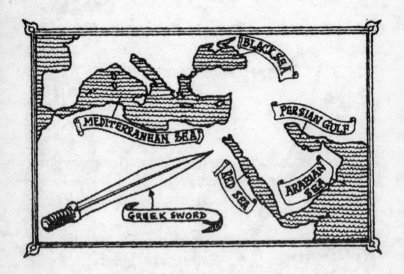

WHO WERE THEY? Mainly Greeks and North Africans who refused to accept the rule of the Roman Empire.

TYPICAL BOOTY: African grain being shipped to Rome, and any other booty on board, including slaves.

TYPE OF SHIP: They used galleys, rowed by oarsmen. The galley often had a ram for bashing the victims' ship.

TYPICAL WEAPONS: Swords and catapults. The Romans dreaded the early Arab corsairs in the Red Sea

DISTINGUISHING FEATURES: They had an intense dislike of Romans.

NASTY HABITS: They liked to bow, sarcastically, in front of Roman captives and then make them jump in the sea, sneering, "You can go home now!"

GREATEST SUCCESS: In 67 BC they looted Ostia, the port of Rome, and 400 other towns. They were so powerful that they controlled most of the Mediterranean.

WORST DISASTER: They were devastated by General Pompey and his navy for looting Ostia in 67 BC.

GREATEST RECOVERY: Sixty-six years after recovering from Pompey's purge, pirates brought Rome to the verge of starvation by blockading the ports.

HOW THEY WERE PUNISHED: Crucifixion. This was the Roman way of dealing with pirates, rebels and Christians. The victims often had to carry their cross to the place of execution. A small wooden ledge on the cross held up much of the weight of the body but their hands and feet were nailed or roped to the cross.

A fearsome
galley
gangster

NASTY NORTHMEN

WHEN? 700 – 950

WHERE? Baltic Sea, North Sea and a lot of the Black Sea, Mediterranean and Atlantic.

WHO WERE THEY? Vikings – small-time farmers from Scandinavia who got bored in summer.

TYPICAL VICTIM: Irish monks, Russians, Saxons – anyone living near the coast.

TYPE OF SHIP: Their longships usually had a fearsome figurehead and woolly sail. They were rowed by up to one hundred oarsmen.

TYPE OF WEAPON: Broadsword, axe and firebrand.

DISTINGUISHING FEATURES: They were tall, with fair hair. Usually bearded.

NASTY HABITS: They liked looting and pillaging. Sometimes they cut the hamstrings of their captives to make sure they didn't escape. Some captives were blinded or skinned alive.

GREATEST SUCCESS: The conquest of Britain, Normandy, Ireland and the burning of Paris in AD 911. Christians who expected to be attacked added an extra line to their prayers: "From the fury of the Northmen, Good Lord, deliver us". Vikings also reached Sicily and North Africa, and helped to found Russia. The Normans, led by William the Conqueror, who conquered England in 1066, were descended from the Vikings.

WORST DISASTER: They were defeated by Alfred, King of Wessex, at the Battle of Edington in AD 878.

MOST FAMOUS NORSE PIRATE: Erik the Red, murderer, who discovered Greenland.

Erik the Red c. 950–1010

A figurehead was the carved figure on the prow of the ship.

MEDIEVAL MUGGERS

WHEN? 1000 – 1485

WHERE? All around Britain, the North Sea, Atlantic and a bit in the Mediterranean.

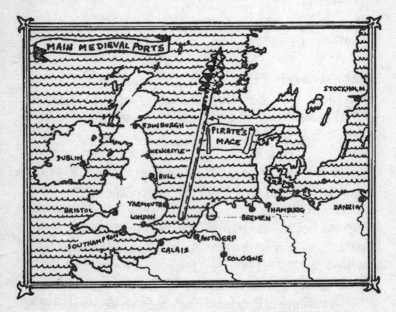

MAIN MEDIEVAL PORTS

PIRATE'S MACE

STOCKHOLM
EDINBURGH
NEWCASTLE
DUBLIN
HULL
YARMOUTH
BRISTOL
LONDON
HAMBURG
DANZIG
BREMEN
SOUTHAMPTON
ANTWERP
CALAIS
COLOGNE

WHO WERE THEY? Pretty well any sailor and any outlaw looking to cash in on growing international trade.

TYPICAL VICTIM: They attacked merchant ships carrying fish, wine, coal, and wealthy knights who they could kidnap and hold to ransom.

TYPE OF WEAPONS: Sword, dagger, mace, arrows.

TYPE OF SHIP: Cogs, or round-ships.

DISTINGUISHING FEATURES: None at all – could be anyone.

NASTY HABITS: Torture.

GREATEST SUCCESS: They secured near complete freedom of the seas for themselves. For years, no one could stop them.

HOW THEY WERE PUNISHED: Execution – they might be hung or disembowelled.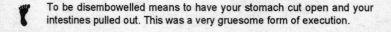

MOST FAMOUS MEDIEVAL MUGGERS: The Victual Brothers. This was an alliance formed after 1241 against the German merchant towns of the Hanseatic League. Originally the Victual Brothers were themselves part of the Hanseatic League, but the lure of easy money turned them against their former friends. They adopted the motto, 'Friends of God and enemies of the world', which makes their attitude pretty clear. For years they plundered ports and shipping lanes, but were finally defeated and executed by the merchants in 1402.

A one-eyed medieval mugger

To be disembowelled means to have your stomach cut open and your intestines pulled out. This was a very gruesome form of execution.

CRAZY CORSAIRS

WHEN? 1300 – 1800

WHERE? Mostly around the coasts and islands of the Mediterranean.

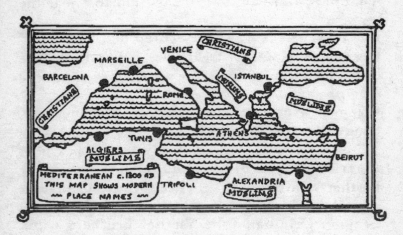

WHO WERE THEY? Christians and Muslims.

TYPE OF WEAPONS: swords, scimitars, pistols and cannon.

ARAB SCIMITARS

TYPE OF SHIP: Usually large galleys, or small galleys called galliots.

NASTY HABITS: Muslims: beating slave oarsmen with a whip made from a dried elephant's penis. Christians: chopping slaves in half if they got too near the rudder.

GREATEST SUCCESS: They learned to build the European round-ship for sailing beyond the Mediterranean.

WORST DISASTER: From the 1730s, the leading European countries signed peace treaties which allowed their navies to help each other against the pirates. But when the navies of England and Holland were busy fighting Napoleon, corsairs prospered again.

MOST FAMOUS CORSAIRS:

The Knights of St John were descendants of the old Christian crusaders. The Barbary corsairs were Arab pirates, their bitter enemies. However both sides attacked ships of all countries. One famous Arab corsair was Arouj Barbarossa.

Barbary coast corsair

EARLY PRIVATEERS

WHEN? 1520 – 1600

WHERE? They were active all over the place but especially in the Spanish Main.

WHO WERE THEY? Sailors from north European countries.

HOW THEY WERE PUNISHED: By hanging or beheading.

DISTINGUISHING FEATURES: A privateer vessel behaved much like an ordinary pirate-ship, but the captain carried a 'Letter of Marque.'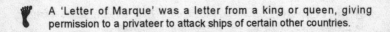

A 'Letter of Marque' was a letter from a king or queen, giving permission to a privateer to attack ships of certain other countries.

Type of weapon: Cannon, and swords for hand to hand fighting.

17th century ship's cannon

Typical victim: Spanish treasure galleons returning to Spain from the Americas.

Greatest success: In 1572 Drake led a raid against the treasure-port of Nombre de Dios and made off with enough treasure to build and equip thirty warships.

Nasty habits: They tended to attack any ship and not just the enemy.

Type of ship: Galleons, caravels, pinnaces.

Most famous privateer: English hero Sir Francis Drake.

Sir Francis Drake
1540-96

 You can see a picture of a galleon in the 'Stealthy Ships' chapter. Caravels and pinnaces were early types of galleon.

BLOODY BUCCANEERS

WHEN? 1523 – 1720

WHERE? The Spanish Main.

BUCCANEER REGIONS
YUMA ISLAND
ATLANTIC OCEAN
CROOKED ISLAND
MAYAGUANA
ACKLIN'S ISLAND
CAICOS ISLANDS
TURKS ISLANDS
CUBA
GREAT INAGUA
LITTLE INAGUA
SILVER BANK
GUANTANAMO
TORTUGA ISLAND
SANTIAGO DE CUBA
PORT DE PAIX
HISPANIOLA
PORT AU PRINCE
MONTEGO BAY
JAMAICA
PORT ROYAL
CARIBBEAN SEA

WHO WERE THEY? Originally they were French settlers and a mixed bunch of English, Dutch, Welsh and Irish. They were sometimes called 'picaroons', from a Spanish word meaning 'mischief-maker.'

TYPICAL VICTIM: A Spaniard.

TYPE OF SHIP: At first hollowed-out tree trunks, then anything they could capture – preferably fast sloops.

DISTINGUISHING FEATURES: They stank of meat, and tobacco spiced with gunpowder. Often drank too much alcohol. Wore round caps and linen breeches. Clothes stiff with blood from slaughtered beasts.

TYPE OF WEAPON: Cannon, cutlass, pistol, musket, hunting knife.

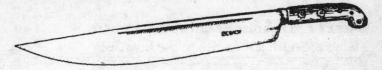

Buccaneer's hunting-knife

NASTY HABITS: Killing any Spaniard they met, even ordinary seamen.

HOW THEY WERE PUNISHED: Hanged, decapitated or enslaved.

MOST FAMOUS BUCCANEER: Blackbeard – the craziest pirate of all.

A buccaneer or 'boucanier'

HOW THE BUCCANEERS GOT THEIR NAME

Jean Florin, a French pirate, captured three Spanish treasure ships in 1523. The Spanish responded by trying to clear the Caribbean islands of all peoples including the French settlers. The settlers were called 'boucaniers' because they barbecued or dried their meat on a wooden frame called a 'boucan'. These 'boucaniers' responded to the Spanish attacks by attacking the Spanish ships. They were so successful they took it up full time.

BEASTS OF THE EAST

WHEN? 1700 – 1900

WHERE? Arabian Sea, Indian Ocean, Straits of Malacca, South China Sea to the Java Sea.

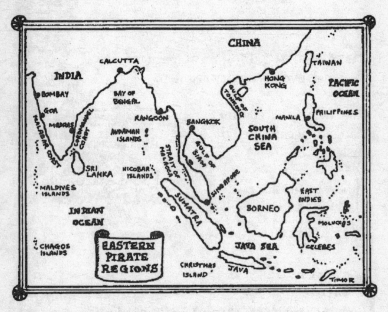

EASTERN PIRATE REGIONS

WHO WERE THEY?
Arabs, Indians, Dyaks, Chinese, Malays.

TYPICAL VICTIM: An East Indiaman sailing back to England loaded with cotton or tea.

TYPE OF BOAT: Arab dhows, Chinese junks, sometimes galleys.

DISTINGUISHING FEATURES: Love of loot, dislike of hard work.

NASTY HABITS: Chinese pirates would carry the heads of their victims strung round their necks by their pigtails.

TYPE OF WEAPON: guns, curved swords such as the scimitar or the kris, bows and arrows, daggers.

Eastern pirate

Malay kris

GREATEST SUCCESS: Ching was a dwarf Chinese fisherman who commanded a fleet of six hundred pirate junks until his death in 1807. The fleet was divided into six squadrons, each flying a flag of a different colour. The largest ships carried twelve guns and rowboats. Each rowboat could hold twenty men and carried swivel guns.

GREATEST DISASTER: Kanhoji Angria built up a chain of twenty-six pirate ports on the Malabar coast, robbing the merchant ships of the British East India Company. In 1755 Commodore William James sailed in close under the guns of four of the forts and bombarded the pirates for two days, until the gunpowder store in one of them exploded. This was the end of the Angria brigade.

HOW THEY WERE PUNISHED: The Chinese liked to nail a captured pirate's feet to the deck, then beat him with sticks.

AVAST THERE, LANDLUBBERS! FEAST YER EYES ON OLD EBENEZER'S NEWS SCRAPBOOK!

DAILY CUTLASS

1550

Circulation 50,000 pirates

BUTTOCK SHOCK FOR BUCCANEER

Louis le Golif, the buccaneer, has had one of his buttocks blown away by a Spanish cannon ball. He is now known as Borgne-Fesse or 'Half Arse'.

Rumour has it that le Golif is writing his memoirs, which promise to tell of one pirate he once knew called 'the Exterminator' (real name Montbar de Languedoc) who had eyebrows bigger than his moustache.

BUTCHER GOES OUT WITH A BANG   1818

Rahmah Bin Gabr, the Barbary pirate better known as the Butcher Chief, has died in battle — but not without taking his enemies with him.

Aged 70 and blind as a bat, the Butcher Chief has been at war with his great rival Suleiman, the Sheikh of Bahrain.

Relying on a slave to know how the battle was going, the Butcher Chief blew up his own boat after Suleiman's men had climbed aboard. All on board were killed.

BOTTLES SAVE BART

Buccaneer Bartholomew Portuguez has escaped from being hanged by the Spanish by stabbing his guard to death and jumping overboard.

Unable to swim, he took two big bottles with him to keep him afloat till he reached land, where he hid for four days in a hollow tree.

Just desserts, Billy 1240

William March, the English pirate, was arrested while eating his dinner on Lundy Island in the Bristol Channel.

For many years March has captured wealthy merchants and held them to ransom. However, he overstepped the mark when he tried to have English King Henry III assassinated.

DAILY CUTLASS

6 June 1530   Circulation 50,000 Pirates

Carry on crusading

The famous Knights of St John have taken over Malta as a base for pirate operations against Muslim ships.

Their pirate expeditions are called corsos, and so pirates in the area are now known as 'corsairs'.

Stomp 'em, Pomp! 66 BC

Pompey, the great Roman commander, has cleaned up the Med in record time. In just 40 days, his 270 ships have captured 400 pirate ships and destroyed 1300 others.

10,000 pirates have been killed and 20,000 taken prisoner. The new tough approach follows the looting of Ostia, Rome's main port, by pirates. The pirates have been grabbing Baltic timber, Spanish timber, British tin and grain from Egypt, bringing Rome to the brink of starvation.

Punk Monk Sunk 1217

The French pirate, Eustace the Monk, has paid with his head for leading an invasion of England.

In the fierce battle of Sandwich, Eustace's French soldiers were showered with lime which made their eyes water. While they were wiping them Eustace was captured and executed.

His head, stuck on the end of a pole, is currently touring the main towns in the south of England.

JULIUS CAESAR AND THE PIRATES

Remember Julius Caesar who invaded England in 55 BC? Well, in 78 BC he was captured by pirates from Asia Minor (now Turkey). Spotting him as a very important person, they put a ransom of 25 silver pieces on his head. Caesar was outraged. "I'm worth at least double that!" he declared. "OK" replied the pirates, "50 silver pieces".

It took Caesar's men almost six weeks to raise the cash, by which time the pirates were glad to see the back of him. He never stopped complaining and saying how he would crucify the pirates when he was set free. He spent his time having his hair cut (his personal barber was with him) and writing awful poems which he inflicted on the pirates. Caesar was true to his word. He raised an army and had the pirates caught and crucified. But because they had treated him so well, he allowed them to have their throats cut before being nailed to their crosses.

BETWEEN DECKS

A REALLY NIFFY CHAPTER

Pirate ships were disgusting places. They stank of bad food, damp clothes and rotten stuff called bilge water sloshing about in the bottom of the ship. Imagine an old, wet dog steaming in front of a fire and you will get the general idea. Pirates were niffy. They hardly ever washed. There were no toilets. Pirates just squatted over a hole – called the heads – in the bow of the ship, then washed it down with buckets of sea water.

Pirates never changed their clothes for weeks. One Barbary corsair called The Butcher Chief wore his until they were rags – which couldn't have been much fun for his two hundred wives! If you could stand the smell, and weren't too picky about the table manners of your shipmates or washing, or anything else civilized, you could have a great time. You'd have to really want to be a pirate though! Read on...

THE PIRATE CREW

Pirate ships needed huge numbers of men to capture other ships. A merchant vessel intended for a crew of twenty might carry a hundred pirates.

Pirate officers were elected by the crew and, if the crew later found they didn't like the officers, the crew booted them out. Apart from the captain and officers, skilled sailors such as carpenters and gunners, known as 'sea artists', also received an extra share of the loot, but only if they took the risks too. 'Artists' who didn't fight had to make do with a lower share. Musicians were specially important. The pirate orchestra used to strike up a really terrifying din when a pirate ship went into the attack.

Because pirates didn't like anyone thinking they were better than they were themselves, officers were given no privileges other than a bigger share of the booty. Only the captain had his own cabin. Even so, the crew could just barge in and eat the dinner off his plate if they wanted to.

Pirates could just barge in and help themselves.

PIRATE DISEASES

There wasn't room for everyone below decks, and anyway it was so smelly that pirates slept packed like sardines on deck. Sleeping so close together and being so dirty meant that diseases spread like wildfire, and they caught all sorts of things. What with the dirt, the crowded conditions and the bad eating habits, disease might finish off half a ship's crew on a long voyage. This is why pirate captains like to choose 'seasoned' crewmen who had caught and recovered from diseases such as yellow fever.

Raw recruits were sometimes left on a disease ridden island for a season of three or more months to become 'seasoned'. Too bad if they died in the meantime! In fact pirates were such a sickly lot that the first booty they went for on captured ships was often the medicine chest.

Scurvy, caused by a lack of vitamins, was commonplace. It made gums go rotten, loosened teeth and caused stinky breath. Legs became twisted out of shape. People died in extreme cases. The cure for scurvy was fresh fruit, which was difficult to get.

PICK A SICKNESS

YOU'RE SICK...MAYBE DYING...AARGH!

If you had to be a poorly pirate, which of these disgusting diseases would you choose to have?

GANGRENE – rotting flesh

MALARIA – fever, seeing things

YELLOW FEVER – yellow skin, vomiting, death

TYPHUS – sweating, vomiting, the runs, death

So what did pirates do all day?

When they had done the hard work like getting supplies aboard, rigging up the sails and generally getting everything ship-shape, pirate life could sometimes get a bit boring. Pirates often just got drunk, swore a lot and told tall tales. Some played cards and dice – all day and every day. If there was a pirate orchestra aboard, the men would dance with each other. Women were rarely allowed aboard in case the men fought over them.

One favourite game was to act out being caught and tried. These mock trials were called Pirate Pantomimes. In 1717 one pirate took it so seriously that when he was found guilty he bombed the mock-jury and cut off the arm of the prosecutor, a pirate called Alexander the Great.

Rules

Pirate rules were called Articles, and were a written list which men signed when they joined a pirate crew. They swore over a Bible or an axe, promising to obey the rules on pain of death. The Articles covered things like punishments, behaviour aboard ship, hours of work and the sharing out of booty. Despite all the rules, pirate ships were mostly in a state of crazy chaos because every pirate felt he ought to be the boss. Here are some of the strict rules drawn up by the crew of the *Revenge*, captained by John Phillips about 1700. Notice that the captain only gets a bit more money than members of his crew.

- ☠ Every man shall obey civil command: the captain shall have one full share and a half in all prizes: the carpenter, boatswain and gunner shall have one share and a quarter.

- ☠ If any man shall offer to run away or keep any secret from the company, he shall be marooned, with one bottle of powder, one bottle of water, one small arm, and gunshot.

- ☠ Any man that shall strike another whilst these articles are in force shall receive Moses' Law (that is thirty-nine lashes with a whip) on the bare back.

- ☠ Any man that shall not keep his arms clean, fit for an engagement, or neglect his business, shall be cut off from his share and suffer such other punishments the captain and company think fit.

PIRATICAL COOKING
(FOOD ABOARD SHIP WAS USUALLY HORRIBLE!)

☠ Stale water was often kept in scummy, rotten barrels, so pirates drank rum with everything. For a change they might drink some captured brandy. All this alcohol pickled their livers. A pickled liver could lead to jaundice.

☠ Meat was smoked and was as tough as old boots. When Henry Morgan's men marched on Panama they ran out of meat, so they soaked, roasted and ate leather bags abandoned by the Spanish.

☠ Ships' biscuits were so full of worms, weevils and biscuit beetles that they were best eaten in the dark! Sometimes they were soaked in rum and brown sugar then boiled up and eaten like porridge (along with the weevils!).

☠ There were no ships' cats left aboard pirate vessels after a long voyage. Cats made too tempting a meal for them to live long. Besides – cats catch rats and eat them. What a waste! Rats made a smashing roasted snack!

☠ When pirates did get fresh meat, they went mad. It all went in the pot: skin, feathers, shell, beak and all. This delicious stew, livened up with fish, eggs, onions and red-hot peppers, was called Solomon Grundy.

Jaundice – condition caused by obstruction of the bile which results in a yellowish skin colouring. Bile is a horrid yellow-green fluid produced by the liver.

TWO FAVOURITE PIRATE RECIPES
PIRATE STEW AND PIRATE BREW

PIRATE STEW – SOLOMON GRUNDY

INGREDIENTS:

skin
feathers
beak
lots of peppers

METHOD:

mix it all together,
simmer for a long
time and...enjoy!

PIRATE BREW – KILL DEVIL

INGREDIENTS:

rum
wine
tea
milk
lime juice
sugar and spices

METHOD:

mix it up and pour
down the throat
...AHHH!

PIRATICAL PUNISHMENTS

DID THEY REALLY WALK THE PLANK?

The life of a seaman was harsh and often brutal. Punishments aboard all ships were pretty horrible, so piratical punishments weren't that much worse than many others. Imagine being stripped naked, tied to a rope, and pulled

YUMMY YUM! DINNERTIME!!

beneath a ship, and back again. The sharp barnacles scrape and tear your skin. Salt-water gets into the cuts. It brings tears to the eyes just to think about it. Called keel-hauling, this punishment started in Roman times. Originally, keel-hauling wasn't a punishment at all; it was a job. Someone was pulled under the ship to clean the hull – necessary on long voyages. Another punishment was being flogged with a cat o'nine tails. This was a stick with nine knotted tails of a rope attached to it. Pirates hated flogging so much that they often banned it on their own ships.

WALKING THE PLANK

Walking the plank was the pirate-punishment that never was – almost. One of the few times it may have happened was in 1769. A sailor called George Ward was in Newgate jail waiting to be hung for mutiny on the high seas. He confessed to the prison chaplain that he and his fellow mutineers had made several non-mutineer sailors 'walk on a plank extended from the ship's side, over the sea, into which they were turned, when at the extreme end'.

Ward may have made this all up. On the other hand, he may have heard about this trick being done in 1700 by a ship's carpenter, the Danish pirate Derdrake. He was always angry and is said to have made people walk the plank to cheer himself up.

We often think that making captured prisoners walk the plank was a typical pirate thing to do, even if it never really happened. But they had plenty of other ways of torturing and disposing of enemies...

The most serious thing a pirate could do wrong aboard a ship was to be a coward or to fall asleep on lookout. Since both of these could cost the lives of their shipmates, the punishment was death. Shooting, being thrown into the sea, or being covered in hot tar and feathers were popular methods of punishment or execution.

Another fun thing some pirates got up to was to haul a prisoner high into a rigging – then suddenly let go. The victim crashed to the deck while the drunken onlookers roared with laughter.

Captain Cobham was an English pirate who hated the Spanish. When he captured one Spanish galleon he found badly-treated English prisoners in the hold. In a fit of rage, Cobham had the entire Spanish crew sewn up in their mainsail and thrown into the sea.

CAP'N'S CHOICE

Imagine you're a pirate captain. One of your crew has been caught stealing some booty from a fellow crew member. You need to make an example of him to impress your crew. Which punishment will you chose?

CHOICES:
1. Make him walk the plank.
2. Drag him behind the ship.
3. Tell him off.
4. Slit his ears and nose.
5. Maroon him on a desert island.
6. Slit his ears and nose and maroon him.

MAROONING

Another popular piratical punishment was marooning. Pirates found guilty of theft from their companions or of desertion were often cast adrift in a small boat, or marooned on an uninhabited island, with just a bottle of water, a gun, and some ammunition. Few victims survived.

SWEATING

A circle of candles was lit around the mast where it passed through a lower deck. The victim then had to scurry round and round the mast as he was prodded with cutlasses and forks.

After about ten minutes most victims would collapse with heat exhaustion. They would be dragged away and replaced by a fresh prisoner.

For threatening an officer, a pirate might have his hand cut off. For robbing a fellow pirate, the offender could have his nose and ears slit. Chinese pirates could have their eardrums burst for going ashore without permission.

Facing death bravely!

When facing execution themselves, some pirates were as tough as nails. One pirate waiting to be hanged in 1718 was asked to repent by someone in the crowd. "Yes" he replied, "I do heartily repent. I repent I had not done more mischief and that we did not cut the throats of them that took us. And I am extremely sorry that you aren't hanged as well as we are!"

THE STORY OF ROBINSON CRUSOE

Robinson Crusoe *is the famous story about a man who was shipwrecked on a desert island. The story is based on the real life story of Alexander Selkirk, the son of a Scottish shoemaker. Young Selkirk ran away to sea after being accused of bad behaviour in church.*

By 1702, Selkirk was serving as sailing master on one of the ships in the fleet of William Dampier. Dampier was a buccaneer and explorer, who was to get into trouble for being cowardly, brutal and drunk.

Selkirk and Dampier didn't get on, and eventually they had a nasty argument. Selkirk asked to be set ashore on one of the Juan Fernandez islands off the coast of Chile. They left him there with clothes, bedding, gunpowder, bullets, tobacco, a hatchet, a knife, a kettle, a Bible, some instruments and books.

At the last moment Selkirk changed his mind and begged to rejoin the ship, but Dampier put a damper on that idea. They sailed away without him.

Poor old Selkirk survived for five years. In 1709 he was eventually found by an English privateer ship captained by Woodes Rogers. Selkirk was dressed in goatskins and looked wild. Dampier was actually on board this ship, but by now he was a humble pilot.

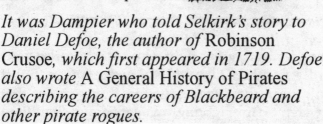

It was Dampier who told Selkirk's story to Daniel Defoe, the author of Robinson Crusoe, *which first appeared in 1719. Defoe also wrote* A General History of Pirates *describing the careers of Blackbeard and other pirate rogues.*

ATTACK!

GRAPESHOT AND GRAPPLING IRONS

HIT AND RUN

Pirates were really hit and run raiders. Lookouts at the top of a 100 foot mast could spot a prize from twenty miles away. So, too, pirate ships could be spotted by a merchantman or gunboat. One thing you simply didn't do was fall asleep on lookout duty. Your shipmates might just chuck you overboard!

Pirates preferred not to fight. Does that surprise you? It hardly fits their bloodthirsty pirate image. But it doesn't mean they were cowards. It just shows that they weren't daft. Fighting was dangerous. Shot fired from a cannon could maim and kill. Oak splinters the size of daggers could turn a pirate into a dead pin cushion. He might be peppered with pistol shot, hacked with an axe, slashed by a sabre or cut by a cutlass. Worst of all, he might not be dead and so he would have to suffer the not so tender loving care of the ship's surgeon or carpenter!

How Pirates Planned an Attack

Plan A: Speed

Pirates were careful not to attack heavily armed ships. They would track a prize for hours, even days, to make sure it could be taken easily. Pirate sloops were quicker and nippier than heavy merchantmen. They could dodge the cannon fire, whilst pirate marksmen tried to pick off the enemy gunners. Once under the stern, they wedged the rudder with their bows to prevent the prize escaping. Then they boarded using grappling ropes, called creepers, and boarding nets.

Plan B: Cunning

Pirates tried all sorts of tricks. They used log boats or canoes at night to creep up to ships at anchor. They flew fake flags to fool the prize into thinking they were friendly. They pretended to be harmless merchantmen.

Plan C: Terror

If neither speed nor stealth did the trick then plan C was put in place. They tried to frighten the crew of the prize into giving up. A warning shot might be fired; pirates were careful not to sink the prize with the booty still aboard. Just to increase the pressure, the pirate orchestra played like a sackful of yowling cats, while pirates danced like madmen, waving cutlasses and screaming threats. But all of this might be unnecessary, since most seamen's legs turned to jelly when the Jolly Roger was run up.

The classic skull and crossbones

THE FLAGS PIRATES FLEW

A French pirate flew the first black flag in 1700 during a fight with an English man-of-war off Jamaica. The flag had crossed bones with a death's head. Sometimes, an hourglass symbolized time running out for the victims.

Where the name 'Jolly Roger' came from is a mystery. French sailors flew a red flag known as a 'joli rouge', which sounds rather like 'Jolly Roger'. Another story tells of a Tamil pirate from India called Ali Raja. He flew a red flag which English pirates called Ally Roger's flag. 'Ally' could have changed to 'Jolly'.

'Black Bart' Roberts' Flag

ABH AMH

Two other explanations are to do with the nature of pirates. 'Old Roger' was a popular name for the devil. Also, 'Roger' was an old English word meaning a vagabond rogue. Take your pick.

Some pirate captains adapted the Jolly Roger to their own design.

'Calico Jack' Rackam's flag

'Black Bart' Roberts pictured himself standing with each foot upon a skull. One was labelled ABH (A Barbadian's Head) and AMH (A Martinician's Head). This symbolized his hatred for the governors of Barbados and Martinique, who were out to get him.

'Calico Jack' Rackam had a skull with crossed cutlasses. Some ships flew a black flag with a skeleton holding a tankard of rum in one hand and a cutlass in the other.

The idea of all these ferocious flags was to terrify merchantmen. By reminding them about death they hoped to scare them into surrendering. Pirates preferred to get hold of the booty without a fight and this was one way to do it. But if they did have to fight, they made sure they were well prepared.

Skeleton and tankard flag

Pirates fired lots of different kinds of shot at their prizes:

THE MUSKET was too long to use when boarding but was fine for picking off targets at long range.

THE "BROWN BESS" FLINTLOCK MUSKET

THREE IRON DISCS attached by chains to a fourth. Killed and maimed anyone standing in the way.

A ROUND BALL with large hooks was used to tear sails and rigging.

The musket and the blunderbuss worked on the same system as the flintlock pistol, which was used for close quarters fighting.

THE BLUNDERBUSS was a medium-range scatter gun filled with lead shot, nails or even gravel. It was used for firing at a crowd of deck hands.

BLUNDERBUSS

GRAPPLING IRONS, or hooks, were used for pulling down sails, holding ships together — and as a very vicious weapon.

Other long range weapons included iron or granite cannonballs and grenades filled with nails and iron scraps. The grenades were meant to rip people to pieces.

Smelly stink pots filled with lit sulphur were used to blind and choke. Grapeshot was small iron balls packed together which scattered when fired: meant to maim. Rockets, called serpents, were used to frighten the enemy. One captain who ran out of grapeshot while attacking a prize used gold coins instead! After the battle his surgeons had to remove the coins from the victims' bodies.

THE WEAPONS PIRATES USED:

CLOSE RANGE

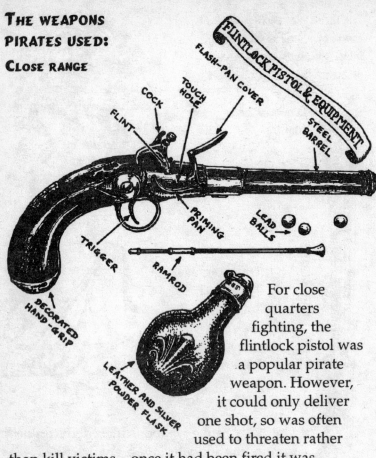

FLINTLOCK PISTOL & EQUIPMENT

FLASH-PAN COVER

TOUCH HOLE

COCK

FLINT

STEEL BARREL

PRIMING PAN

LEAD BALLS

TRIGGER

RAMROD

DECORATED HAND-GRIP

LEATHER AND SILVER POWDER FLASK

For close quarters fighting, the flintlock pistol was a popular pirate weapon. However, it could only deliver one shot, so was often used to threaten rather than kill victims – once it had been fired it was useless, except as a cosh! It took a skilled pirate maybe 30 seconds to reload and fire. He had to:

1. Unstop the powder flask.
2. Pour powder into the barrel.
3. Stuff the powder down with the ramrod.
4. Drop in a ball.
5. Ram the ball into place.
6. Lift the flash-pan cover.
7. Pour powder into the flash-pan.
8. Replace the flash-pan cover.
9. Pull back the cock.
10. Take aim and pull the trigger.

By the time he'd done all this the enemy could be hacking him to pieces. That's why most pirates carried two guns and an arsenal of other weapons – a cutlass, a dagger and a boarding axe.

SHORT DAGGER

BOARDING AXE

A BOARDING AXE was used to cut rigging, and smash doors and barricades.

THE DAGGER was used for close quarters fighting.

Once aboard, pirates fought like demons without regard for their own lives, perhaps because they were often drunk. As well as their daggers for stabbing, and boarding axes for clearing away obstructions, pirates also used pikes for impaling and chopping, and cutlasses for slashing at their victims.

HOW TO RESIST A PIRATE ATTACK

Pirates didn't have it all their own way. If the crew kept their heads, an armed merchantman with only eighty men on board could easily be defended against up to two hundred pirates. An eighteenth century handbook advised captains to order their crews to barricade themselves in the forecastle, or the great cabin, if their ship was in danger of being boarded by pirates. Once they were barricaded in, it was very difficult for the pirates to get them out, even if the pirates had control of the open deck. Only very heavy gunfire or a battering ram could dislodge them. However, if the pirates plundered the ship and set it alight before leaving, the crew of the merchantman would would be stuck.

One way of protecting your merchant ship from pirate attack was to travel in a convoy with other merchantmen. But pirates would sometimes take advantage of this situation; they would set an old hulk on fire and let it drift into the convoy of merchant ships. In the confusion and panic they could then sneak in and pick off one or two of the more vulnerable ships.

Sometimes the attacked crew would leave a booby trap on deck. They would hide out of sight after laying a trail of gunpowder to a powder chest full of nails and scrap iron. When the pirates boarded, the crew would light the fuse and run for the safety of the great cabin, or the forecastle.

AFTER THE FIGHT...

Once the fighting was over there was usually lots of blood to mop up. Sometimes the surviving victims were made to mop it up. Badly injured men were unlikely to live for long afterwards. A bottle of rum was the only pain killer available. Limbs were cut off by the surgeon with a crude saw. The carpenter did the job if no surgeon was available.

Stumps of amputated limbs were plastered with boiling tar to stop the bleeding. The shock of this treatment was often enough to kill the patients. Gangrene or other infections finished off most of the rest.

CAN YOU SPOT THE DIFFERENCE BETWEEN THE PIRATE SURGEON AND THE PIRATE CARPENTER?

THE SURGEON

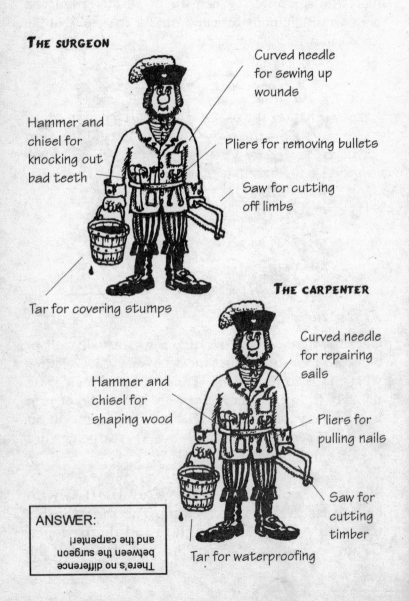

Curved needle for sewing up wounds

Hammer and chisel for knocking out bad teeth

Pliers for removing bullets

Saw for cutting off limbs

Tar for covering stumps

THE CARPENTER

Curved needle for repairing sails

Hammer and chisel for shaping wood

Pliers for pulling nails

Saw for cutting timber

Tar for waterproofing

ANSWER:
There's no difference between the surgeon and the carpenter!

56

If a pirate managed to survive surgery, but was disabled, he was usually well looked after...

A pirate with a hook hand might be given easy jobs to do - perhaps as a cook.

He might get an extra share of loot. On Henry Morgan's expedition to Jamaica in 1670, the ship's articles allowed for generous compensation to pirates injured while fighting. These included:

100 Spanish dollars for an eye

600 Spanish dollars for the loss of a leg

1800 Spanish dollars for both legs

When cash was short, slaves might be used as compensation.

CAPTAIN HOOK

'Peter Pan' is a strange pirate story written by J. M. Barrie in 1904 and made into a famous cartoon film in 1953. It features the dreaded pirate character, Captain Hook.

Peter Pan is a boy who never grows up. he lives in the magical Neverland where the 'lost boys' who fall out of their prams end up. He takes Wendy Darling and her brothers to a fantasy island where they are caught up in a fight with a desperate pirate band led by Captain James Hook.

His dastardly assistant, Mr Smee, calls his cutlass 'Johnny Corkscrew' because he likes to wiggle it round in his victims' wounds! Hook's a bit of an oddball too – a harpsichord-playing ex-public-school boy turned sea rover. He likes to think he's a gentleman, but everyone's scared of his scheming ways, his nasty temper and his vicious steel hook. He and Peter Pan are deadly enemies, because Peter had cut off Hook's hand and fed it to a crocodile!

TICK! TOCK!

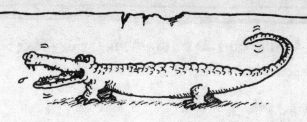

Hook's afraid of the crocodile – it's had a taste of Hook's flesh and wants the rest of him. Luckily for Hook the crocodile swallowed a clock so he knows when the beast is following him because it ticks.

Hook captures Wendy and the boys and takes them to his filthy ship, the 'Jolly Roger'. Here he offers them a choice – be cabin boys or walk the plank. The brave boys refuse to be pirates so Hook gleefully gets his plank ready. But... Peter comes to the rescue, ticking like the crocodile to frighten off Hook. While Hook's hiding, Peter unties the captives and, in the fight that follows, kills off most of Hook's vile crew. Peter and Captain Hook clash in an epic sword fight which only ends when Peter kicks Hook off the side of the ship. And guess what's waiting below? The crocodile! Aaargh!

A MINI-QUIZ ALL ABOUT PIRATE ATTACKS

Are these statements true or false?

1) A pirate on lookout could spot a prize twenty miles away.

2) Pirates loved fighting, and never missed an opportunity for a good scrap.

3) Pirate weapons included grenades and rockets.

4) All pirate ships flew a skull and crossbones flag.

5) Captain Hook was eaten by a large fish.

6) Surgery for pirates wounded in battle was painful but safe.

DON'T WORRY ME LAD – IT WON'T HURT A BIT!

ER... CAN'T I JUST HAVE A PLASTER?

ANSWERS:

1) True, see page 46.

2) False, see page 46.

3) True, see page 51.

4) False, see page 49.

5) False, see page 58.

6) Definitely false! See page 55.

PIECES OF EIGHT

BOOTY, BULLION, AND BURIED TREASURE

Booty, also called plunder or prize, was what being a pirate was all about. Booty was not just treasure chests, stuffed with gold. Pirates had to be content with whatever their victims were carrying. They weren't fussy. Here's some of the booty taken by the pirate Edward Davis in the 1680s:

- 5 bags of assorted silver plate and coins
- 4 pairs of silk stockings
- 2 paper books
- several pieces of ribbon

Other booty might include tobacco or rolls of cloth. Alcohol was common booty, which was why pirates were often drunk. In 1399, the townsfolk of Dartmouth were drunk for a week on French wine brought back by pirate captain John Hawley. All 1500 barrels of it! Pirates from Hastings were hung in 1769 for robbing a Dutch coaster of sixty hats. Calico Jack Rackam was such a bad pirate that his booty was often just ships' ropes, sailcloth or fish.

Robbing the *Samuel* off the north American coast in 1720, even the great 'Black Bart' Roberts had to be satisfied with capturing sails and a chap called Harry Glaser who was the Chief Mate. People were often regarded as booty. Captives might be held to ransom. Sea artists – skilled sailors such as navigators and gunners – were captured and added to the pirate crew.

Sometimes pirates got it wrong. In 1681 four hundred ingots of silver taken from the *Santo Rosario* were mistaken for tin and dumped overboard. Shiver me timbers!

Ships were booty. If one fitted the bill, it was either swapped for the pirates' ship or just added to the pirate fleet. In 1717, Blackbeard captured a French merchantman and renamed it *Queen Anne's Revenge*. Sometimes ships were booty in more senses than one; the German pirate Kapitan Stortebeker, who was captured in 1402, was said to have had a ship with a golden mast. A chunk of it was made into a golden crown for the spire of St Nicholas's church in Hamburg. But cash was what pirates wanted most of all. These are some of the most common coins of the seventeenth and eighteenth centuries:

✴ Ducats (Denmark) ✴ Louis D'Ors (France) ✴
Shillings (England) ✴ Guineas (England) ✴
Crowns (England) ✴ Crusadoes
(Portugal) ✴ Doubloons (Spain)
✴ Pieces of Eight
(Spain) ✴ Daalders
(Holland) ✴ Mohurs
(India) ✴ Deniers
(France) ✴

MIDDLEMEN

The booty captured by pirates was only valuable if they could trade it for cash. Middlemen provided this service. In 1700 it was estimated that the American colonies earned one billion pounds, in today's money, in ten years of dealing with pirates. Middlemen were expert in trading in stolen booty, which was often far cheaper than legal goods.

Ten days after a Dutch vessel was robbed off the Cornish coast in the 1500s, her cargo of linen was being sold in London shops. That's fast!

TREASURE TROVES

Successful pirates could become very greedy and sometimes very rich. It was hard to know what to do with all their loot. If they didn't drink it all away, then they had to keep it somewhere secret, away from other pirates. Sometimes they buried it.

There's a lot of buried treasure waiting to be found even now.

I WONDER IF THERE'S ANY TREASURE BURIED AROUND HERE?..

Cocos Island is said to have three hoards of treasure, buried by Captains Thompson, Edward Davis and Bonito Benito at different times. Thousands of people have tried to find it and failed, and Cocos Island is only three miles square. What does that tell you? Either the treasure is very well hidden, or there is no treasure, or, perhaps, it has already been found and nobody said a word.

Robert Louis Stevenson based his book *Treasure Island* on some real treasure he had heard about. In the book, Stevenson kept the name of the real place a secret because he was going to search for it himself – at La Plata, off the coast of Ecuador. Stevenson never found it, but somebody else did.

The treasure, dropped by Sir Francis Drake into fifteen metres of water in 1578, was found in 1930.

The process of burying treasure must have been very risky. After all, anyone who knew where it was could come back later and dig it up. Blackbeard had a thing about leaving his wives (alive or dead, it didn't matter to him) to guard his buried treasure. In 1715 he left his fourteenth wife (yes, fourteenth – most of the others met a grisly death) to guard his treasure on London Island, off the New England coast. She died in 1753 but her ghost is said to guard it still.

CAPTAIN KIDD'S TREASURE

Everything went wrong on Captain Kidd's voyage of 1695-8. He was an English privateer who meant to get rich by capturing pirate ships and French ships. The trouble was that he couldn't find any of these.

He had no luck at all. On one ship he did capture, all he found was a bale of pepper and a sack of coffee. On another ship, he only got some tubs of candy and another sack of coffee.

Eventually, he struck lucky with a ship called the Quedah Merchant, *and stole a rich haul including lots of jewels, silver and gold, not realising that the ship's captain was English. He was now in big trouble. From then on the English merchant ships treated him as a pirate while the other pirate ships continued to treat him as an enemy.*

Eventually, he sailed home to New York. He buried his treasure at Gardiner's Island, to the east of Long Island and in other places. But then he was captured by the governor, Lord Bellomont.

Lord Bellomont promised to help Kidd, if he told him where he'd buried his treasure. Kidd told him, and Bellomont searched frantically for it. On Gardiner's Island they found 1,111 ounces of gold, 2,353 ounces of silver and 1 lb of precious stones. It was all sent back to England.

Kidd was hung. Two of his co-defendants, Nicholas Churchill and James Howe, paid the Newgate jailers £315 for their release, and they sailed past Kidd's gibbet and across the Atlantic to Pennsylvania where they dug up £2,300 of gold from one of Kidd's hoards. It is said that there may be more of Captain Kidd's booty still waiting to be found.

CAPTAIN AVERY AND THE EXCEEDING TREASURE

The best booty of all was carried by the ships of the Grand Moghul sailing from Arabia to India. The richest prize ever was taken by Englishman John Avery (or Long Ben Avery or Henry Every, if you like: he used different names). In 1695 he captured "the greatest ship in all the dominions" of Emperor Aurangzeb, the Grand Moghul of India. The ship was well named. It was called Exceeding Treasure *and carried 500,000 gold and silver coins. It lay heavy upon the water, crammed with silver and gold, jewels and silks. The raid made every pirate aboard as rich as a lottery winner. As you can imagine, the Moghul didn't feel quite so grand about it. Hating the English, he ordered his boys to rough up the East India Company's trading post, looting enough to more than cover the loss. The East India Company, in turn, put a price of £500 on Avery's head.*

PIRATES IN PORT

RUM AND GUNPOWDER, WINE, WOMEN AND SONG

Pirates did not live all their lives at sea. For one thing it would have been dead boring. For another, they would have had nowhere  to spend their loot. There is little point in robbing ships if you can't show off afterwards. They liked nothing better than swanking around town in fancy clothes glittering with gold and jewels. They spent fortunes on drink, gambling and women.

Men who weren't drunk were viewed with deep suspicion – there must be something wrong with them!

Brandy was the most popular pirate drink on the Spanish Main, but rum was much easier to get hold of. Originally called rumbullion, rum was nicknamed Kill Devil. It certainly saw many pirates to an early grave. Some pirates drank a cocktail of rum, wine, tea, milk, lime juice, sugar and spices all mixed together. Little wonder pirates had terrible bowel problems. Blackbeard's favourite tipple was an explosive mix of rum and gunpowder.

Pirates could spend the equivalent of an ordinary seaman's lifetime wages on drink within a few days or weeks, returning to sea to refill their purses when they were skint. The tavern keepers, whose coffers were bursting with pirate cash, would not hesitate to sell the pirates into slavery if they fell into debt.

But pirates couldn't go just anywhere. They ran the risk of having their 'necks stretched' (being hanged). They needed to feel safe from arrest, so they looked for isolated islands and secret creeks and coves where they could hole up and also clean their ships.

COME ON IN, JAKE! THE WATER'S FINE!

CAN'T! I'LL GET WORMS IN ME PEG LEG!

Cleaning the ship was a complicated business called 'careening'. The wooden hull had to be scraped clean of weeds, and greased to prevent them growing back. The grease also helped stop a pest, the terrible teredo worm, from eating the hull. The ship was beached and laid on its side for cleaning. While a ship was being careened the crew were stuck on land and vulnerable to attack.

Life-size teredo worm

There were many pirate havens, but some of them deserve a special mention:

PIRATE HAVEN 1: NEW PROVIDENCE

Pirates chose islands like New Providence in the Bahamas, which was ruled for a time by a council of pirate captains as if it were a ship. If food and fresh water were plentiful, shanty towns like Nassau in New Providence grew up. The houses were made from driftwood and palms, or upturned rowing boats. Taverns and other shops were built of driftwood and sailcloth.

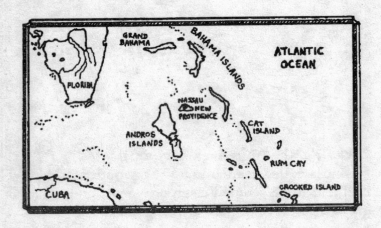

PIRATE HAVEN 2: RHODE ISLAND

Other pirate havens were found on the mainland of America where governors would be friendly towards pirates in exchange for a piece of the action, or a bribe. On Rhode Island, the pirate chief Thomas Tew was often seen travelling in the governor's carriage. The people of Rhode Island made a handsome living building and supplying pirate ships.

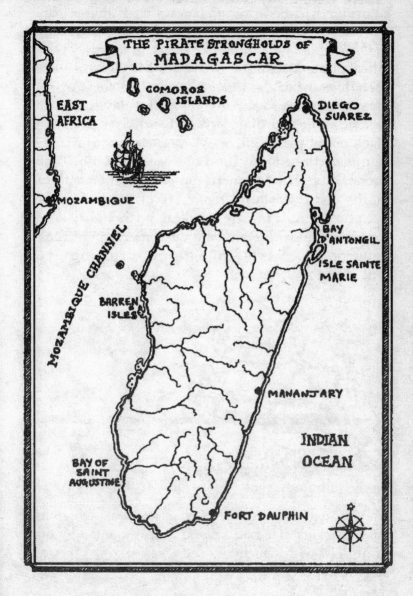

THE PIRATE STRONGHOLDS OF
MADAGASCAR

St Mary's Island near Madagascar was a port and

trading station, run by Adam Baldridge in the 1660s. Baldridge had fled from Jamaica after killing a man. He was one of several pirates who set up trading stations which they ruled like kings. In fact they were called pirate kings. The natives of Madagascar were friendly most of the time, except when some of the pirates took to capturing them for slaves! Adam Baldridge kept a diary which is why we know so much about pirate life on Madagascar. At St Mary's he traded pirate booty for meat, vegetables, flour and ammunition. Huge cannons protected the pirate ships in the little harbour from attack and massive warehouses were jam-packed with booty and supplies. Baldridge's pirate customers spent their days on St Mary's sunbathing, drinking and canoodling with women.

Another ex-buccaneer on Madagascar was known as 'Old Crackers'. He had several guns mounted by his front door with which he fired a salute when pirates arrived in port.

Other pirate characters on Madagascar included John Plantain, King of Ranter Bay. He went to war over the granddaughter of a native chief called King Dick. Plantain kept many native African wives, whom he renamed with English names like Moll, Sue or Peggy.

PIRATE HAVEN 4: LIBERTALIA

The most famous pirate haven of all was Libertalia, also on Madagascar. It was made famous by Captain Johnson in his book *A History of Pirates*, which was published in the 1700s. He wrote that Libertalia was founded by a pirate called Captain Mission in 1709. It had shops, a church and a meeting place where the pirates agreed on decisions to be taken. The pirates lived in neat white houses with gardens. They grew crops and made things to sell. It all sounded too good to be true – and it was. Captain Johnson made it all up!

LIBERTALIA FLOWER-
ARRANGING AND
BIBLE-READING CLUB

PIRATE HAVEN 5: SCILLY ISLES

Lord High Admiral Sir Thomas Seymour was so keen to become a pirate that he *bought* a safe haven! He set up his own pirate base in the Scilly Isles (off Cornwall) in the early 1540s after getting fed up with the English government's feeble efforts to fight the Spanish.

PIRATE HAVEN 6: PORT ROYAL

Today, Port Royal in Jamaica is a small fishing village. It is hard to imagine that only 300 years ago it was twice the size of New York (New York, then, that is!) and was one of the richest towns in the world. The wealth came from piracy. Letters of marque were issued by the Governor, letting Port Royal's pirates plunder Spanish ships.

Over six thousand people lived at Port Royal. Besides pirates, buccaneers and slaves, the population

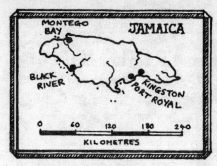

included merchants, goldsmiths, doctors, tailors, carpenters and of course, tavern keepers. The town had the reputation of being the 'cesspool of Christendom'. Fortunes were won and lost in the gambling dens. Women were bought and sold like second-hand cars.

The pirates of Port Royal invented no end of ways to have fun. Dutch pirate chief Roche Braziliano used to set up a butt of wine in the main street. People who refused to take a drink with him were shot. Another time he set up a cask of butter and threw handfuls of it at people.

A favourite Port Royal sport was called 'sparrow shooting'. The 'sparrow' was a slave or, better still, a Spaniard, who was fastened by a chain to a stake. The chain was long enough to enable him to jump out of the way of bullets fired at him by pirates. Points were awarded for hitting particular parts of his body.

Another jolly Jamaican sport was shark-sticking. For a bet, or just for a dare, a pirate would wade out from shore and wait for a shark to arrive. The idea was to stab the shark to death with a dagger before it started eating his legs. Pirates who succeeded were heroes who then drank themselves legless. Pirates who failed were just...legless!

GOD'S RETRIBUTION

Port Royal was the most notorious place on earth. When pirates dreamed, it was said, they dreamed not of heaven but of Port Royal. What happened on the 7th June, 1692, was thought by many to be a punishment from God. At twenty minutes to noon the town shook as the earth moved. Buildings fell down and warehouses slid into the sea. But that was only the start. A huge tidal wave swept in from the Caribbean and as the sea returned it took two thirds of the town with it. Two thousand people died later from fever and disease. Although rebuilt, Port Royal was never the same after that. Today, a Jamaican legend tells how on still nights the church bells can be heard from the sea bed, rung by the ghosts of the drowned pirates.

STEALTHY SHIPS

HOW TO SPOT A PIRATE SHIP

From the earliest days of piracy, the ships used by pirates have been all shapes and sizes, but they have generally been chosen for speed and easy handling. Hit and run is the name of the pirate game. Slip up to the treasure ship, slap the crew about and slope off with the treasure. He who hits and runs away, lives to rob another day.

DHOWS: FROM 2000 BC

An Arab ship with a triangular sail, used for sailing the Red Sea, Arabian Sea and Indian Ocean.

ARMAMENTS: Light cannon

MAX SPEED: 10 knots

MAX LENGTH: 10 m

MAX CREW: 50

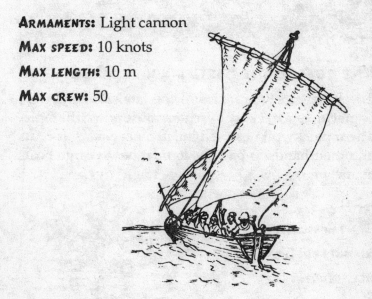

GALLEYS: 1500 BC – AD 1850

These ships were used by some of the heroes of the Greek legends as well as by pirates. They could have up to five banks of oars, and were rowed by slaves. They were well suited to the often smooth waters of the Mediterranean. They could easily row up to becalmed sailing ships. Some had a bronze ram for bashing merchant ships before boarding.

ARMAMENTS: Bow ram, catapults, cannon later

MAX SPEED: 12 knots

MAX LENGTH: 40m

MAX CREW: 200

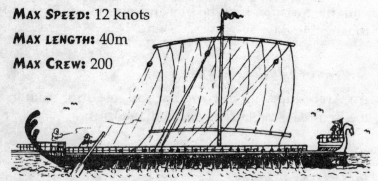

NILE GOAT BOATS: STARTING ABOUT 50 BC

The Egyptian Pharoahs and the later Romans were sometimes attacked by river raiders on the Nile. These plucky pirates used inflated goat skins as boats and their hands as paddles to float out to cargo boats at anchor.

ARMAMENTS: Dagger

MAX SPEED: Slow

MAX LENGTH: 1m

MAX CREW: 1

CHINESE JUNKS: 2000 BC – 20TH CENTURY

ARMAMENTS: Originally swordsmen, cannon later

MAX SPEED: 12 knots

MAX LENGTH: 40m

MAX CREW: 200

A light flat bottomed ship without a keel, upright prow or upright stern. The hull is split into watertight sections, which make the ship strong and safe. It has a heavy steering oar or rudder. The sails are made up of narrow horizontal strips of matting or linen. Pirates favour small, flat junks for swift attack and get-away.

LONGSHIPS: 7TH-11TH CENTURIES

The long boat used by the Norsemen was fast and fearsome. There was a fierce figurehead at the front, which could be detached on entering a friendly harbour. The ships were rowed by Viking warriors, who were famous for their strength and violent antics. A woolly sail helped to push the ship along if the wind was in the right direction. Good for sailing into shallow water to attack coastal villages.

ARMAMENTS: Axemen!

MAX SPEED: 10 knots

MAX LENGTH: 46m

MAX CREW: 60

COG: MEDIEVAL, 12TH – 15TH CENTURIES

ARMAMENTS: Archers, later cannon

MAX SPEED: 8 knots

MAX LENGTH: 30m

MAX CREW: 30

The cog, or round ship, was developed by German and Dutch ship-builders for sailing in the rough waters of the North Sea and the Baltic Sea. Its shape made it hard to capsize and left plenty of room for cargo. Pirates stood on the 'castle' at the back and hurled spears and arrows at the crews of merchantmen.

THE GALLEON: 16TH – 18TH CENTURIES

ARMAMENTS: Heavy and light cannon

MAX SPEED: 8 knots

MAX LENGTH: 43m

MAX CREW: 320

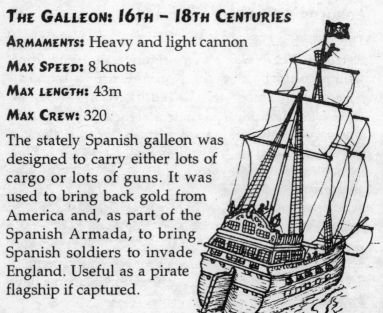

The stately Spanish galleon was designed to carry either lots of cargo or lots of guns. It was used to bring back gold from America and, as part of the Spanish Armada, to bring Spanish soldiers to invade England. Useful as a pirate flagship if captured.

SLOOP 17TH AND 18TH CENTURY

The sloop was small but really fast, just right for chasing bigger ships over open sea and hiding in narrow creeks. With all that sail and light weight the sloop was a superb racer, the ultimate pirate ship.

ARMAMENTS: 14 light cannon

MAX SPEED: 12 knots

MAX LENGTH: 22m

MAX CREW: 75

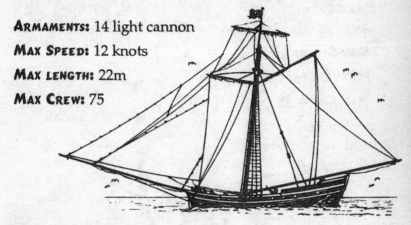

SQUARE-RIGGER: 19TH CENTURY

ARMAMENTS: 20 cannon, swivel guns

MAX SPEED: 8 knots

MAX LENGTH: 30m

MAX CREW: 200

The three masted square-rigger took over from the galleon as queen of the seas. It was slow but could carry heavy loads over long distances. If loaded with cargo, the pirates loved to attack them. Fitted with guns, a square-rigger could take on a navy frigate. Good as a pirate flagship.

SCHOONER: 19th-20th century

The two masted schooner combined size and speed, and so made an ideal ship for pirates. She was also popular because of her shallow draft, which made it easy to sail into rocky coves to hide.

ARMAMENTS: 12 cannon, swivel guns

MAX SPEED: 11 knots

MAX LENGTH: 30m

MAX CREW: 75

Women Pirates

A Brutal Bevy Of Buxom Buccaneers

If you think women never went to sea, but just sat at home like little Miss Muffet, you're way off target. Some of the most gruesome girls ever to walk the planet have taken to piracy – and enjoyed it.

Women were never normally allowed aboard a pirate or naval ship at sea, as this was thought to be unlucky. This may have just been due to the usual suspicious nature of the most sailors. But experienced captains also knew that lonely men, sometimes at sea for months on end, could easily start fights over a woman.

However, some captains were known to smuggle a girlfriend on board disguised as a cabin-boy. And women sometimes dressed as men in order to lead an adventurous life, and so got aboard under false pretences.

In the Middle Ages, aristocratic women might take charge of the male crew of a ship. Alvilda the Goth was unusual in having an all-woman crew.

The Goths were a wild tribe of warriors and sailors, originally from Eastern Europe.

Buxom Buccaneer No. 1: Alvilda the Goth

The Goths were North Sea pirates even before the Vikings got started. Alvilda's father, Sypardus, the King of Sweden, wanted her to marry a prince of Denmark called Alf. She hated this idea, so she ran away to sea with a bunch of other wild women and set up as a pirate. Eventually their raids got out of hand and the authorities decided to act. As chance would have it, it was Alf who was sent to sort them out. He didn't know that Alvilda was the chief pirate but when he captured her ship he was so taken by her that he proposed. This time Alvilda accepted, and they got married.

BUXOM BUCCANEER NO. 2: JEAN DE BALLEVILLE

Jean was a twelfth-century noblewoman from Brittany (now part of modern-day France). She took to the sea with three ships after her husband was wrongly executed. She made sure that she was always the first to board captured ships.

BUXOM BUCCANEER NO. 3: MARY READ

Mary Read was born in 1692. When she was a young girl, her single-parent mother struggled to make ends meet. Eventually, Mary's mother hit on the idea of asking for help from Mary's grandma. There was only one problem – grandma hated little girls. So Mary Read had to be dressed up and presented to her grandma as a little boy. This worked – but ever after, Mary Read had a taste for boyish adventure, preferring to be a boy rather than a girl.

She joined the Royal Navy when she was thirteen. Later she fought as a soldier in Flanders, and fell in love with a cavalry man. They married and set up a pub together but, sadly, Mary's husband died. Heartbroken, she sailed to the Caribbean in a Dutch merchantman, using the name Mark Read. On the way, her ship was captured by the pirate Calico Jack Rackam. He offered Mary a place in his crew, which she willingly accepted.

BUXOM BUCCANEER NO. 4: ANNE BONNY

Meanwhile, Anne Bonny, the daughter of a rich Irish planter, had run away from home in Carolina to marry a poor sailor. Anne developed a fancy for pirate captains, but not Blackbeard. He was so smelly that she rejected him, saying she would "sooner kiss a pig". In 1719, she fell in love with Captain Calico Jack Rackam, left her husband, and sailed aboard Rackam's pirate ship. Later that year Rackam captured the merchantman on which Mary Read was a sailor. Bonny also wore mens' clothes; this was the only way that her lover, Captain Rackam could get her on board. Mary Read fell in love with Bonny, thinking 'him' a handsome sailor. However, they soon discovered each other's secret! That's how Mary Read and Anne Bonny teamed up to become the world's most famous female pirate duo.

They proved to be the bravest fighters on Calico Jack's ship. When it was captured by the King's men only the two women and one man stayed on deck. All the rest, including Calico Jack himself, fled and hid below decks in terror.

The two women were spared hanging because they both claimed to be pregnant. Calico Jack, though, was less fortunate. He was hanged! Before the execution took place, Anne visited him and told him, "If you had fought like a man you need not now be hanged like a dog". Tough cookie, Anne Bonny!

BUXOM BUCCANEER NO. 5: MARIA COBHAM

Maria Cobham, who sailed with her husband, was as bloodthirsty a pirate as you could be unlucky enough to meet. She liked to tie her captives up in sacks and throw them overboard. She also roped officers to the mast and used them for target practice, and she once poisoned the entire crew of a captured Indiaman. Maria and her husband eventually built up a great fortune in plunder and were able to retire to a private estate on the coast of Northern France. They became very respectable, and Captain Cobham even became a magistrate. But it's said that they once came out of retirement to capture a merchant ship which had foolishly anchored near their private harbour. Once a pirate – always a pirate.

Buxom Buccaneer No 6: Grace O'Malley

Grace O'Malley was a sixteenth-century pirate married to two West of Ireland chieftains. In her spare time she was also a pirate chief in her own right; she ran a fleet of pirate ships from Clare Island in Clew Bay. Feeling her age a bit when she was fifty-six, she visited Queen Elizabeth I to ask for a pardon. The Queen and Grace are said to have got on well. They both loved the sea and the Queen was happy to grant Grace her wish. Grace O'Malley retired with her memories to a life of luxury in her castle overlooking the sea.

Buxom Buccaneer No 7: Ching Yih Saou

Ching Yih Saou, also known as Mrs Ching, was one of the most successful pirates of all time. She was the widow of the pirate admiral Ching who drowned in 1807 when his ship sank in a typhoon. After he died, Mrs Ching took over and expanded the family business to 800 war junks and over 1000 smaller ones. In all, she commanded over seventy thousand pirates: men, women and children.

Mrs Ching had a thing about chopping people's

heads off. Chopping offences included going ashore a second time without permission (the punishment for doing it once was having holes cut in the ears), stealing booty from the rest of the crew (everything captured was written down in a book), cowardice and molesting women.

Mrs Ching had hundreds of boyfriends, But one man she really took a fancy to was Richard Glasspoole. She kept him on deck in a wooden cage and fed him with rice and caterpillars, but, perhaps not surprisingly, he couldn't bring himself to be friendly back! When Mrs Ching saw she was getting nowhere with Glasspoole, she ransomed him for $7,654, some opium, some silk and a telescope.

At that time the British government offered rewards for the capture of pirates. Twenty dollars was given for every head. Mrs Ching's crafty pirates took along the heads of innocent settlers, sometimes six at a time, tied by their pigtails and slung round the pirates' necks, and claimed the rewards. Mrs Ching finally bribed the Chinese governor into giving her a pardon. She then became a smuggler.

COULD YOU BE A BUXOM BUCCANEER?

1. Imagine you're walking down a quiet street and you see a small child drop a packet of sweets, do you...

   a) Grab the sweets and run?
   b) Pick them up and give them to the child?
   c) Grab the sweets, empty them down the drain and watch the child cry?

2. Your parents give you £20 to buy a new dress. Do you..

   a) Buy a nice pretty dress?
   b) Buy a beefburger and chips, then get some popcorn and go to the cinema?
   c) Spend the money on a pair of boxing gloves or a swiss army knife?

3. The school bully beats up your best friend. Do you..

   a) Tell your teacher about the bully?
   b) Laugh?
   c) Hide in the nearest toilet?

ANSWERS:

Correct pirate answers: 1) a   2) c   3) b

Score 10 points for each right answer.

0 points – much too nice to be a good pirate!

10 points – a slight trace of wickedness, but not nearly enough.

20 points – not bad, or rather, quite bad but not bad enough!

30 points – wicked! Anne Bonny – you ain't seen nothing yet...

TOP TEN PIRATES

THE SHADIEST SAILORS ON THE SEVEN SEAS

Pirates came in all shapes and sizes – and most of them were crazy characters. Here are ten of the most outlandish outlaws of the sea...

THE MOST SUCCESSFUL

Roberts didn't want to join the pirates when he was first captured by them but soon changed his mind when he was elected captain. Once he had turned pirate, Bartholomew 'Black Bart' Roberts captured 400 ships in the four years between 1718 and 1722. He turned his crews into rich men.

'Black Bart' was particularly brutal towards Spanish prisoners from Martinique. The Governor of Bermuda wrote to London in 1720, complaining that the prisoners were "barbarously abused, some were almost whipped to death, others had their ears cut off, others they fixed to the yardarm and fired at them."

He was also famous for being a non-drinker and preferred tea to alcohol – very unusual for a pirate! He died of a gunshot wound in 1722.

Black Bart Roberts

THE MOST COLOURFUL

John Rackam was called 'Calico Jack' on account of his clothes which were bright calico cotton. He was unusual because he allowed the famous female duo Anne Bonny and Mary Read on board his ship. Women were almost never allowed to sail with pirate crews.

THE MOST BLOODTHIRSTY

Picture a man who cuts hearts out of Spaniards and chews on them to get others to talk. Picture also a man who chops Spaniards' heads off and licks his sword after each head rolls to the deck. Picture that and you have the cruellest and most bloodthirsty pirate afloat. Francois L'Olonnais, a French buccaneer in the 1660s, was not a nice man to know, especially if you were Spanish.

Francois L'Olonnais

THE MOST WICKEDLY SWINDLED

After his capture of the
Grand Moghul's ship
Exceeding Treasure in 1696,
Captain Avery was
swindled of his booty by
shifty Bristol merchants.
He probably died a
pauper in Bideford,
Devon. Some say he is
buried under a headstone
inscribed, 'Captain
Bridgman'. But is he?

Some say he escaped to Madagascar to
live like a king with a captured Indian princess.

THE MOST MISUNDERSTOOD

William Dampier had the
reputation of a bold, bad
pirate. In fact he collected
animals and plants and
wrote about them and
about the places he'd
visited during his three
voyages around the
world. At sea, he kept his
notes dry by putting them
inside bamboo poles

which he sealed at the ends with wax. Dampier
probably never made any money as a pirate,
although some say he buried a fortune somewhere
in Northern Australia.

THE MOST HEROIC

To the Americans, John Paul Jones was a hero. To the British, he was a nasty pirate who kept sinking British ships or taking them as prizes. During the American War of Independence, he had the cheek to sail the coastline of Britain, raiding at will. Try as they might, the Royal Navy could not catch him. In 1779, he fought an especially fearsome battle with HMS *Serpis*. Things got so hot that the *Serpis* gunners were found roasted at their cannons. Only their collars and wristbands remained on their charred bodies.

WAAAH!! PUT ME OUT!!

THE GREATEST TURNCOAT

Sir Henry Mainwaring (1587-1653) was a vice admiral and a pirate hunter. He turned pirate when he joined the Barbary corsairs in 1612. Four years later he changed his mind, got a royal pardon and wrote a book denouncing the evils of piracy.

Edward Teach is the most famous pirate ever. You probably know him better as Blackbeard. Teach was a giant of a man, with arms that reached past his knees. He curled his filthy waist-length beard into rats' tails, each tied with pretty silk ribbons. In battle, he wore burning fuses in his hair, giving him the appearance of a devil from hell.

Blackbeard was the most frightening of pirates, with fierce, wild eyes. He had a weird sense of fun. Once, eating with his men, he blew out the candle and fired his pistols under the table at the legs of his fellow diners. When asked why, he said, "If I didn't shoot one of you now and then, you would forget who I am." Blackbeard's favourite game was to invite the toughest of his crew to go below decks with him. Not many dared to refuse. Once below, Blackbeard lit stinkpots of brimstone, sulphur and pitch. The smell was indescribable. As men staggered to the ladder to escape the choking fog, Blackbeard laughed. Mad or what?

THE MOST MERCILESS

Henry Morgan was a buccaneer of the seventeenth century. Given a letter of marque by Oliver Cromwell, he set about plundering Spanish shipping and treasure ports. During his siege of Porto Bello in 1688, he used a human shield of Spanish nuns and priests. When interrogating Spanish captives about hidden gold, his favourite trick was to tie the prisoner down, stretched between four stakes. Then he'd get his men to pile heavy rocks on the victim until he squealed! But as well as being cruel, Morgan was very lucky. The Spanish government complained about Morgan to Charles II, but the British people saw Morgan as a hero. So instead of hanging him, Charles II made Morgan a knight. Sir Henry Morgan became governor of Jamaica – with the job of hunting down buccaneers!

THE MOST INTERESTED IN COOKERY

Edward Low had a reputation for cruelty. He once cut off a captive's lips, toasted them before his face, then made him eat them. After taking two whale boats near Rhode Island, he forced the master of one to eat his own ears, after garnishing them with salt and pepper.

Vanquished Victims

Slaves Of The Waves – And Worse

If pirates captured innocent sailors and travellers, their fate might be anything – death, torture, slavery, or simply being let go. It depended on what the pirates were after. Some pirate captains needed larger crews, so sailors and sea artists were often forced to become pirates – they had no choice. It was either that, or a watery grave, or worse.

Once they worked on a pirate ship, they were outside the law and ran the risk of severe punishment if caught by pirate busters. Sometimes, there were so many of these 'unwilling' pirates, that they might be offered a pardon if they gave up the pirate life.

MARRIED TO A MADMAN

Blackbeard was well known for his cruel antics in keeping his crew in line. But he was a bit of a devil with his victims too. Tales circulated on the American Atlantic coast that he carried a special chopper for

taking the rings off reluctant captives – along with their fingers! It's said that he used the stolen rings for marrying his fourteen wives.

GHASTLY ENDS

Pirates would often resort to torture if they thought their captives had some useful information. Sometimes they wanted to get rid of their captives as fast as possible to stop them talking to pirate busters later. They also wanted to keep up their fearsome reputations. Sometimes they just did it for fun.

EBENEZER PEGG'S MENU OF GHASTLY FATES

Barbecued alive

Made to run the gauntlet round the deck of the ship

Forced to drink large quantities of rum, or brandy, very quickly

Sewn up in sails and tossed overboard

Set adrift in a burning ship

DAILY CUTLASS

Circulation 50,000 Pirates

SPANIARDS SOLD
1560

The Spanish ambassador to London has complained that pirates have auctioned captured Spanish merchants at Dover, accepting £100 for each of them.

The coast is clear
1650

The Emperor of China has ordered his subjects to live inland to avoid the coastal raids of the dreaded pirate Koxinga.

HOLED IN THE HOLD
1832

The Portuguese pirate Benito de Soto, on his ship called *The Black Joke,* captured an English East Indiaman, *The Morning Star.* With his cutlass he savagely killed the captain of *The Morning Star.* Then he locked everyone in the ship's hold, bored holes in the hull and left the ship to sink slowly. Amazingly, the crew got out and saved the ship and themselves. Later, they spotted de Soto on Gibraltar. He was arrested and eventually executed for his crimes.

LIFE SAVINGS
1544

English privateers have attacked a Portuguese ship, the Chagas, which caught fire. Passengers leapt into the sea and were only rescued by pirates if they held up jewels or gold coins.

TIE, DIE

Middle Ages. English and Scottish pirates have taken to torturing prisoners by tying bowstrings round their wrists and private parts before drowning them. Sometimes they also slice off ears and noses.

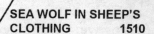

AHOY THERE ME HEARTIES!
HERE'S ANOTHER PEEK AT
OLD EBENEZER'S SCRAPBOOK!

JACK IN A BOX 1806

English sailor John Turner has just been released by Chinese pirates who kept him crammed in a small space measuring just 46 cms by 1.2 metres.

Turner is lucky to be alive. Though he was kicked and beaten, his fellow officers were treated much worse. They had their feet nailed to the deck, or were cut to pieces, or had their hearts eaten.

SMOKED SKIPPER 1822

A captain of the merchantman Mary, captured off Florida, has had both arms cut off at the elbows. He was then placed on a bed of oakum (loose fibre from old ropes) which was soaked in turpentine. His mouth was then filled with the same stuff and he was set alight.

SEA WOLF IN SHEEP'S CLOTHING 1510

The well known Barbary corsairs Arouj Barbarossa and his brother Khair ed Din have come up with another great wheeze in their Mediterranean reign of terror. Spotting two of the Pope's galleys near the island of Elba, the Barbarossas' tiny galliot captured the first galley after a bloody fight. They threw the dead overboard, dressed in the surviving Christians' clothes and sailed the captured galley up to the second Christian ship. Too far off to see the first attack, the unsuspecting Christians in the second galley were easy victims. Most are now slaves of the Africans.

SLAVES OF THE WAVES

Slavery was once common all over the world, and many slaves were used to row galleys. Slaves jumped at the chance to become free pirates but that didn't stop them taking slaves themselves.

Slavery was specially popular in the times of the corsairs. People were the main booty of the corsairs. The wealthy and important they ransomed, and the poor they made slaves.

Slaves were auctioned in slave markets. The lucky ones were bought as household servants. Others broke rocks or built roads. The really unlucky ones were made to row the galleys.

Slaves lived in huge slave towns called bagnios. For those with the cushy jobs, life was not too bad. They might earn money outside of their slavery and own a market stall or café. In time they would probably be ransomed. In the meantime they mixed with other captives, many of whom were seamen or ex-pirates, and they exchanged gossip about the best place to pick up prizes.

In the Algiers bagnio in the 1640s, twenty-two different languages were spoken. So the slaves invented a new language which they all understood.

TURNING TURK

One way a Christian slave could improve his lot was to 'turn Turk'. He had to announce that he was sick of being a Christian and wished to become a Muslim. This got him out of rowing, as Muslims were excused the job of galley slave. Some European seamen turned Turk even without being captured because pay and conditions were better than at home.

Tricking the Turks – by carrying papers saying you were still Christian – resulted in a horrible death. In Barbary ships, most slaves were chained to their oars. The Christians didn't trust their slaves either. A slave approaching the tiller or compass was cut in half and thrown overboard. Christian slaves were usually treated better on Barbary ships because it was a Muslim duty to be 'kind' to slaves. The Maltese Christians had no such scruples. They worked their slaves to death and then just got some more. Life as a galley slave was hard and very, very boring...

PIRATE BUSTERS

HOW PIRATES GOT BUSTED

Imagine you've become a pirate. Lots of booze, booty and sunshine. But don't imagine a happy ending. Piracy was a violent and dangerous trade. Pirates who didn't die of disease or in battle might well end up strung from the yardarm, drowned, chopped to pieces or tortured to death. Take your pick.

The early pirate busters started up around 1700, and by 1720, the golden age of piracy was ended. Then there was a bit of a lull for a hundred years. Pirates found it hard to hide when there were regular navy patrols and strong governors in the colonies. Merchant ships became faster and better armed and there were plenty of ways for seamen to earn a living without taking up piracy. Then, in about 1820, piracy started up again with a vengeance. Navy sailors – out of work after a string of wars had ended – were the main culprits. These pirates weren't the swashbucklers of old. They were cruel and heartless, being as ready to murder for a bag of potatoes as for a bag of gold.

But whenever there have been pirates sailing the seas, there have also been pirate-busters prepared to hunt them down.

PIRATE-BUSTER: WOODES ROGERS

The pirate-buster who cleared the Spanish Main of buccaneers was Woodes Rogers, himself a former privateer. Rogers was made Governor of the Bahamas and told to convert pirates to Christianity and make them mend their ways. He arrived at Nassau, his headquarters in New Providence, in 1718. Word of his appointment had reached pirate ears before he arrived, along with news of the royal pardons that would be given to pirates who reformed. The pirates formed a guard of honour when he stepped off his ship.

HA! YE'LL NOT TAKE ME SO EASY!

One person wasn't having any of it, though. Charles Vane was a pirate and a pirate he intended to remain. He set loose a fireship to cause confusion among the naval force and made good his escape with the Jolly Roger flying.

PIRATE BUSTER: SIR CHALONER OGLE

The hunting down of 'Black Bart' Roberts is a pirate-busting tale almost equal to that of Blackbeard's last stand.

Roberts had been raiding the African Gold Coast at will in his ship the *Royal Fortune*. (Fortune by both name and nature – in 1722 it was so full of treasure that it could barely stay afloat.) The *Royal Fortune* was at anchor in Cape Lopez bay when she was spotted by a naval patrol.

Chaloner Ogle, patrol commander on HMS *Swallow*, moved in for the kill. Roberts' crew was drunk, though the captain himself, being a tea drinker, wasn't. Even when drunk, the pirates were a formidable foe. A great battle ensued. It ended when Roberts was shot in the throat. His men lost their nerve and 169 were captured, of whom fifty-two were hanged. Ogle later became Sir Chaloner Ogle, the only naval officer to be knighted for pirate-busting.

PIRATE BUSTER: CAPTAIN CHAD

In 1835, Captain Chad, helped capture pirates by disguising his ship HMS *Andromache* as a floating zoo. They lined the decks with monkeys, bears and a panther, which so caught the pirates' eyes that they failed to see the twenty-eight guns which were to blast them out of the water.

THE FINAL CURTAIN

Captured pirates could expect little mercy from the law. Romans used to crucify pirates. Greeks tied pirates to stones and threw them overboard. By the time of the buccaneers the most popular form of execution was hanging.

Execution Dock on the River Thames in London was a favourite hanging spot for pirates. Close by was a post from which they were hung in an iron cage after death, their bodies coated in tar to slow down the process of decay. William Kidd's body hung there for years to serve as a warning to all seamen who passed by. His eyes were pecked out by gulls and the body swung in the wind, chains rattling.

Pirates who weren't hung might be tied to a stake at low tide. Onlookers would watch from a distance as the tide came in.

Other methods of execution have been used as well. When the German pirate Klein Henszlein was caught in 1573, he and thirty three of his followers had their heads chopped off. So much blood flowed that it seeped into the executioner's shoes.

Bristol was a wealthy port which attracted pirates who hung out on nearby islands. Lundy Island was an easily defended pirate stronghold for part of the Middle Ages. In 1242 the gentleman rover, Sir William de Manisco, was captured after a raiding spree when based on Lundy. He was taken to the Tower of London and became the first person to be hung, drawn and quartered. This punishment was specially invented for Sir William because he was considered so evil. The victim was hung until nearly dead and then had his bowels drawn out before being cut into four pieces. The head and the 'quarters' were displayed on town walls around the kingdom. Uggh!!

One lot of Medieval Danish pirates – who also preyed on Bristol shipping – didn't do very well. No ships came by whilst they lay in ambush on the small island of Flat Holm, then their own moored boat was sunk by a storm. Stranded on the island they starved to death.

BLACKBEARD'S LAST STAND

The tale of Blackbeard's last stand is one of the most famous in pirate history. In 1718, Blackbeard and his ship were trapped in a narrow creek in North Carolina by pirate buster Lieutenant Robert Maynard, with two naval sloops.

Blackbeard spent the night drinking, and this was to prove a mistake. In the morning, he shouted across at Maynard: 'Damnation seize my soul if I give you quarter, or take any from you'.

Blackbeard ran up a black flag with a death's head on it and then made a break for it. He fired broadside at both naval ships hitting many of the sailors. Maynard ordered the rest of his men below deck. Blackbeard must have thought that he had killed them all and so he boarded Maynard's sloop.

Face to face at last, Blackbeard and Maynard took aim with their pistols and fired at each other. Blackbeard, perhaps because of his night's drinking, missed. Maynard's bullet hit home.

Blackbeard roared and swung his cutlass with such force that Maynard's sword snapped in two. As the pirate moved in for the kill, one of Maynard's men slashed the old rogue across the throat with a sabre.

Blood pumped out from beneath the famous beard, but still the giant pirate fought on and on, until at last he fell like a great wounded bull. When he was finally dead, they counted his wounds. He had twenty five, including five from pistol shots.

Blackbeard's head was cut off and fixed in triumph to the bowsprit of the sloop. The headless corpse was thrown overboard and, so legend has it, swam seven times around the ship before sinking.

Along with Blackbeard ended the golden age of piracy.

CHUI APOO

Much of the great pirate-busting took place during the 1800s in the seas around China and Malaysia. In 1849 a British naval force routed the Chinese pirate fleet of Chui Apoo and his boss Shap-ng-tsai. After a 1000 mile chase, the pirates were cornered in the Tonkin River. Over 2000 pirates were killed, though both Chui Apoo and his boss escaped.

CHARLES GIBBS

A revival of piracy in the Caribbean during the 1820s caused the American government so much trouble that a special US naval patrol was set up. In 1821 they captured four pirate schooners commanded by Charles Gibbs. Gibbs was as 'vicious a rogue as ever sailed'. Gibbs fled into the jungle but, close to starvation, was rescued by an American-bound ship. Unfortunately for him, Gibbs was recognised, tried and hanged in 1831.

ARE YOU NEXT?

WATCH OUT ON THE CROSS-CHANNEL FERRY!

If you thought that piracy on the Seven Seas was dead, think again. Pirates are as almost as active today as were the buccaneers of old. But these days, Spanish galleons and golden doubloons are not the prizes. Instead, pirates are after sea-going casinos and fishing boats, cargo ships, and small boats carrying illegal drugs. Sometimes even oil tankers are diverted and robbed of their cargo. Modern pirates are not the crazed daredevils of the golden age of piracy. Some may be sponsored by corrupt governments or naval officials. It's even been suggested that shipowners sometimes welcome, or even arrange, a pirate attack in order to claim on their insurance.

At least 120 ships are robbed each year by modern pirates. These days, instead of telescopes, sloops and muskets, pirates may use transponders, radar, fast motor boats, automatic weapons and even guided missiles! Thinking of a sailing trip? Are you next?

MODERN MALACCAN MOBSTERS

The waters around Singapore and Indonesia are thick with pirates. Merchant ships leave or enter Singapore harbour every twelve minutes, day and night. Two hundred and forty ships a day pass through the narrow Strait of Malacca. At its narrowest, the strait is barely a mile across. Perfect for pirates! There are so many small craft in the Malacca Strait that the pirates are rarely spotted until they appear on deck.

Malaccan pirates often strike at night and leave quickly. But sometimes they take their time and do a thorough job. The Hai Hui I was carrying 360 tonnes of electronics parts in April 1991. Attacked by armed pirates, the crew were handcuffed and shut in a locker room for four days. The raiders brought another vessel alongside into which they transferred the entire cargo of the Hai Hui I.

In an early conference on piracy in Paris, 1856, several countries refused to sign a declaration against pirates because they were still using privateers to attack their enemies. Among the countries which refused to sign were the United States, Spain and Mexico.

In present day Britain, the Marine Safety Agency issues guidelines on how ships can protect themselves against pirates, and advice about what to do if attacked by pirates. The International Maritime Bureau is a sort of worldwide watchdog which keeps tabs on the state of play in the murky world of modern piracy. It's not just big ships and cargo that go missing. Every year many yachts and small craft vanish. Their crews are never seen again.

When sailing in a known pirate area...

- All crew need to know the anti-attack precautions
- Carry special equipment – extra, hidden radio transmitter, closed–circuit TV, alarm to alert the crew, strong searchlights, night binoculars
- Search the ship for stowaway pirates before sailing
- Avoid talking about valuable cargo over the radio
- 24–hour radio manning, operator to know pirate attack codes
- 24–hour visual and radar lookout
- Stay moving and well offshore until ready to enter a port
- Treat as suspect any small vessel following the ship
- Make quick manoeuvres to swamp boarders' boats
- Water hoses may be used to deter boarders
- Do not use firearms
- Cease resistance if boarders take control of bridge and engine room

Epilogue

You're off on holiday, perhaps on a Caribbean island, or perhaps on the shores of the Mediterranean. The sun is shining down on the white sand and the waves are gently washing the beach. It's a fine day to take a pedal boat and paddle round the bay.

Now that you know all about pirates you know that the Caribbean was once the haunt of Blackbeard and his mates – and the Mediterranean was once a pirate lake infested with corsairs.

But that's all in the past...or is it? That ship on the horizon – look closely at its flag. It's not black is it? Better pedal a bit faster – just in case...

GRAND QUIZ

Now that you've finished this book, why not test your knowledge and find out how good a pirate spotter you'd make? The answers are on page 128.

PART ONE: FAMOUS PIRATES

1) What was a privateer?

a) a secret society which
   wanted to abolish
   private property
b) an especially fierce type of
   Mediterranean pirate
c) a pirate licensed by a
   government to attack enemy shipping

2) Who was Alvilda the Goth?

a) a member of Blackbeard's crew
b) a heavy metal pirate singer
c) an early North Sea pirate

3) Why did Ann Bonny and Mary Read dress as men?

a) because they couldn't find any women's clothing
b) to get on board the all-male pirate ships
c) so they didn't have to cook

4) Who was 'Black Bart' Roberts?

a) a desperate drunken pirate
b) the governor of Martinique
c) a keen tea-drinker

5) What was Blackbeard's real name?

a) Teach
b) Leach
c) Preach

6) What was Blackbeard's
favourite game?

a) skull football
b) synchronized swimming
c) letting off stink bombs between decks

PART TWO: PIRATES ON THE ATTACK

7) Which of these methods were used by
pirates to capture their prey?

a) flying fake flags
b) asking politely
c) using submarines

8) Which of these flags was a pirate flag?

a) a skull and an hourglass on a black
background

b) a skull with crossed pistols

c) a pretty flower

9) Which one of these weapons was not used
by eighteenth-century pirates?

a round ball with big hooks, rockets,
grapeshot, cutlasses, pistols, muskets, land
mines, daggers, grenades.

PART THREE: PIRATE TREASURE

10) How did pirates like spending their ill-gotten gains?

a) repairing church roofs
b) on gambling, drink and new clothes
c) on savings accounts

11) What sort of booty did pirates take?

a) cash only
b) cash plus jewels, gold and silver
c) anything they could carry away

12) Why did pirates bury their treasure?

a) because they didn't trust banks
b) because they liked digging
c) because they wanted to hide it from other pirates

PART FOUR: PIRATE VICTIMS:

13) How did pirates treat their victims?

a) they always let them go
b) they sometimes tortured them
c) they gave them a share of the ship's cargo

14) Why did pirates torture their victims?

a) to get information from them
b) to get a fearsome reputation
c) to have fun

PART FIVE: PIRATE FATES

15) Captain Kidd was...

a) a victim of pirates
b) a well-known pirate buster
c) hung for piracy

16) What was Sir Chaloner Ogle's ship called?

a) the HMS *Swallow*
b) the HMS *Andromache*
c) the HMS *Gulp*

17) Who had his eyes pecked out by gulls?

a) Blackbeard
b) William Kidd
c) Captain Pugwash

 18) Which of these deaths didn't happen to pirates?

hanging, beheading, drowning, gangrene, typhus, over-drinking, starvation after being marooned, malaria, yellow fever, death from wounds obtained in battle

Now
that you've finished my
quiz you'll be wanting to know the
answers, me hearties.
To find out how you've fared in the
pirate-spotter's test, turn to
page 128.
Ha–harr!

INDEX

READ ON

OTHER GREAT BOOKS ABOUT PIRATES

CAP'N SILAS P. THUNDERGUTS' GUIDE TO
PIRATES BY WAYNE N. CABA
Gut-spewing guide to pirates, sea-scum and bilge-rat
buccaneers. A terrifying read. Only for the bravest
readers.

PETER PAN BY J. M. BARRIE
Starring one of the most famous pirates in literature –
Captain James Hook. Pirates capture the Lost Boys of
Neverland and Peter Pan arrives just in time.

PIRATES BY DOUGLAS BOTTING
One of the best books ever written about pirates.
Great illustrations.

PIRATES: FACT AND FICTION BY DAVID CORDINGLY
A good intro to the world of pirates.

BUCCANEERS OF AMERICA BY A. O. EXQUEMELIN
Straight from the (sea) horse's mouth. A reprint of a
French pirate's book written on the Spanish Main at
the time. A real pirate book.

JACK HOLBORN BY LEON GARFIELD
A great pirate tale. Jack stows aboard a ship only to
discover that it is in the hands of really nasty pirates.

A HIGH WIND IN JAMAICA BY RICHARD HUGHES
A gripping read. Emily and her friends are kidnapped
by pirates. Then they run into even deeper water...

THE LADYBIRD BOOK ABOUT PIRATES
BY LAURENCE PEACH
Possibly the best thin book about pirates.

PUGWASH AND THE WRECKERS BY JOHN RYAN
Incompetent Captain Pugwash and his ship *The Black Pig* are constantly being saved by Tom the cabin boy.

AFTER YOU ROBINSON CRUSOE: A PRACTICAL GUIDE FOR A DESERT ISLANDER
BY MACDONALD HASTINGS
A do-it-yourself castaway guide. How would you manage with just a bottle of water, a box of matches and no TV?

OUTCASTS OF THE SEA: PIRATES AND PIRACY
BY EDWARD LUCIE-SMITH
Yo ho ho and a gallon of rum. Forget the glamour. This book gives the real picture, no holds barred.

TREASURE ISLAND BY ROBERT LOUIS STEVENSON
Long John Silver is probably the most famous fictional pirate.

HIDDEN TREASURE BY GEOFFREY TREASE
Think of pirates. Think of desert islands. Think of finding buried treasure. This is the book!

PIRACY TODAY: ROBBERY AND VIOLENCE AT SEA SINCE 1980 BY ROGER VILLAR
You thought that piracy was history. Think again shipmate. It is alive and well.

See if you can find them at your local bookshop or library.

ANSWERS TO GRAND QUIZ

1)	c	see	page 20
2)	c		pages 86
3)	b		page 88
4)	c		page 93
5)	a		page 97
6)	c		page 97
7)	a		page 47
8)	a		page 48
9)	land mines		
10)	b		pages 69 and 75
11)	c		page 61
12)	c		page 64
13)	b		page 99
14)	a, b and c		page 100 (any answer is right!)
15)	c		page 67
16)	a		page 108
17)	b		page 110

18) none of them (trick question!)

Score: 10 points for each correct answer and an extra 40 points if you sussed that 18) was a trick question.

0-100 points: Have you read this book yet?

100-150 points: Pretty good but you guessed at some answers didn't you?

150+ points: Ace pirate spotter!